Crafts for Kids Who Are
LEARNING ABOUT

INSECTS

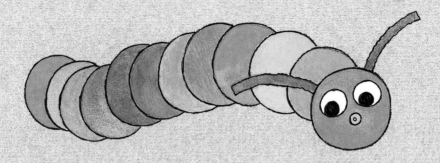

For my new niece, Maia

Millbrook Press
A division of Lerner Publishing Group, Inc.
241 First Avenue North
Minneapolis, Minnesota 55401 U.S.A.

Website address: www.lernerbooks.com

Library of Congress Cataloging-in-Publication Data

Ross, Kathy (Katharine Reynolds), 1948–
    Crafts for kids who are learning about insects / by Kathy Ross;
  illustrated by Jan Barger.
        p.   cm. — (Crafts for kids who are learning about...)
      ISBN: 978–0-8225–7591–7 (lib. bdg. : alk. paper)
      1. Handicraft—Juvenile literature.   2. Insects in art—Juvenile
  literature. I. Barger, Jan, 1948–   II. Title.
TT160.R7125 2009
745.5—dc22   2007001893

Manufactured in the United States of America
1 2 3 4 5 6 – JR – 14 13 12 11 10 09

Crafts for Kids Who Are
LEARNING ABOUT

INSECTS

KATHY ROSS
Illustrated by Jan Barger

M Millbrook Press   Minneapolis

Table of Contents

Bumblebee Change Keeper

Bumblebees are social bees, and this bee wants to hang around with you!

Here is what you need:

narrow black craft ribbon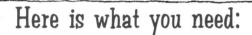

white craft glue

three yellow hinged plastic eggs

two wiggle eyes

scissors

ruler

Here is what you do:

1. Open two of the eggs. Be sure not to break the plastic connectors.

2. Press the longer end of one egg over the longer end of the second. Secure with glue. The open halves form the wings.

3. Cut a 3-foot (90-cm) piece of ribbon.

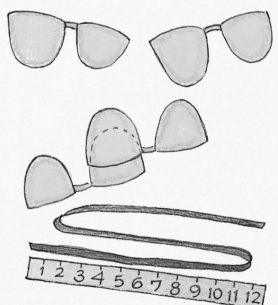

4. Spread glue on the inside of the middle egg section.

5. Press the ribbon ends onto the glue. The ribbon loop will become the hanger.

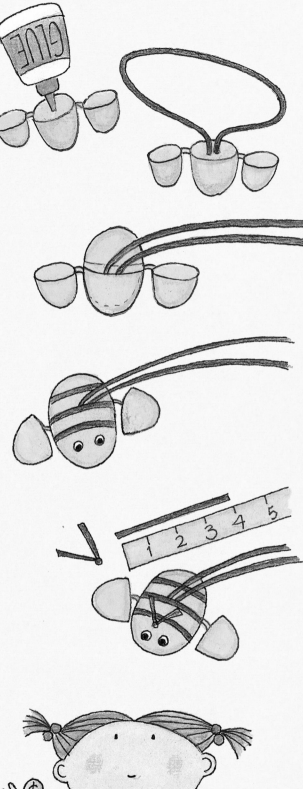

6. Snap the third egg together. Glue the long end of the third egg inside the middle egg section.

7. Cut three pieces of ribbon long enough to go around the bee's body. Secure with glue.

8. Glue on the wiggle eyes.

9. Cut a 4-inch (10-cm) piece of ribbon. Knot the center. Trim the ends. Glue the knot to the top of the bee. These are the bee's antennas.

Open the back of the bee, and stash spare change inside. Snap the egg body shut. Wear the bee around your neck as a necklace. Buzzzzzzzzzzz . . . . .

Bee and Flower Puppet

Bees are attracted to flowers.
Bees eat nectar,
the flowers' sweet liquid.

Here is what you need:

two neckties with a green pattern

discarded colorful necktie

black, yellow, and two green 12-inch (30½-cm) pipe cleaners

white craft glue

two small wiggle eyes

scissors

two round craft magnets

plastic grocery bag

FINE FOOD

ruler

Here is what you do:

1. Cut a 12-inch (30½-cm) piece from the narrow end of the colorful neck tie.

2. Thread a green pipe cleaner through the tie. Gather the tie so that 2 inches (5 cm) of pipe cleaner hangs down. Shape the tie/pipe cleaner into a spiral flower shape. Secure with glue.

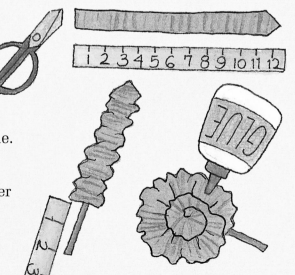

8

3. Bend the pipe cleaner end down. Wrap a second green pipe cleaner around the end of the first. Fold the second stem in half. Twist it around itself to make a sturdy stem.

4. Cut a 3-inch (8-cm) piece from the narrow end of each of the green neckties to make leaves. Glue them to the back of the flower.

5. Glue a magnet to the center of the flower.

6. Wrap the tips of the black and yellow pipe cleaners into a spiral. This is the bee's body. Twist the other ends together. This is the bee stem.

7. Wrap the end of the bee stem into the end of the green stem behind the flower. The bee can bob up and down above the flower.

8. Cut two wings from the plastic bag. Glue them on the back of the bee's body.

9. Place a second magnet on the flower's center. Rub glue on the side that is facing up. Carefully remove the magnet. Place the gluey side on the bee's body. This is the bee's head.

10. Glue on the wiggle eyes.

To use the puppet, hold the stem of the flower and bend the bee forward so the magnets pull the bee to the center of the flower.

Big Bite Mosquito

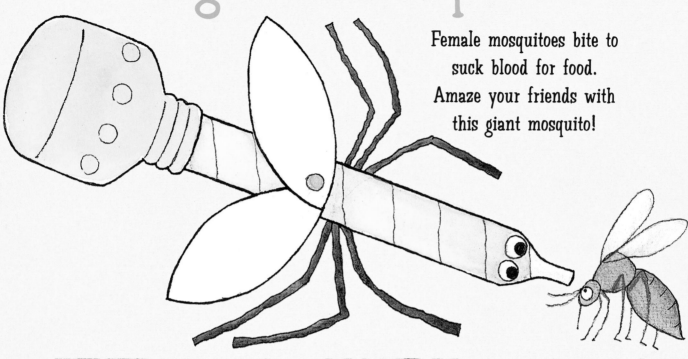

Female mosquitoes bite to suck blood for food. Amaze your friends with this giant mosquito!

Here is what you need:

plastic basting tube

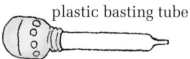

paper cup and craft stick

two white Styrofoam trays

black permanent marker

three 6-inch (15-cm) black pipe cleaners

masking tape

paper fastener

white craft glue

two wiggle eyes

pink sponge

red food coloring

water

scissors

Here is what you do:

1. Wrap three pipe cleaners around the center of the basting tube. Let the ends stick out on each side to form legs.

2. Bend each pipe cleaner in the center to form a knee. Bend each pipe cleaner out on the end to form a foot.

3. Cut two wings from one of the Styrofoam trays.

4. Attach the two wings together using the paper fastener.

5. Tape the end of the paper fastener to the mosquito's back.

6. Wrap the basting tube with masking tape. Leave the narrow end uncovered.

7. Glue the wiggle eyes to the masking tape.

11

8. Mix water with a few drops of red food coloring to make the "blood."

9. Use the marker to draw the outline of a hand on the sponge.

10. Place the sponge in the second Styrofoam tray. Pour the "blood" on the sponge until it is soaked.

To use the mosquito, have it "bite" the sponge hand by squeezing the rubber bulb on the end of the basting tube. Press the open tip into the sponge hand. Slowly release the pressure on the bulb. The mosquito will suck up the blood from the hand just as a real mosquito does.

Aphids and Ladybug Pin

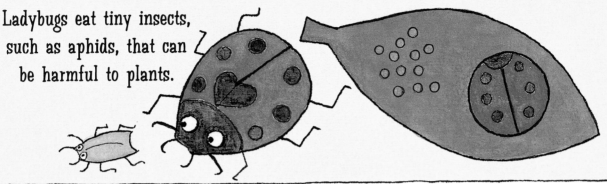

Ladybugs eat tiny insects, such as aphids, that can be harmful to plants.

Here is what you need:

red glass gem (or red craft jewel)

green felt scrap

ruler

black permanent marker

green seed beads

white craft glue

pin back

scissors

Here is what you do:

1. Cut a 3-inch (8-cm) leaf shape from the green felt.

2. Use the marker to draw a head, wing line, and dots on the gem. Glue the ladybug to the leaf.

3. Glue some tiny seed beads to the leaf. These are aphids.

4. Glue the pin back to the back of the leaf.

This pin makes a nice gift for your mom!

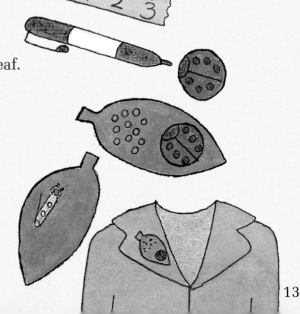

Fly Finger Puppet

That buzzing noise you
hear comes from
a fly beating its
wings very fast.

Here is what you need:

black
stretchy
glove

two small
wiggle eyes

white
craft
glue

two white, blue,
or clear disposable
plastic spoons

scissors

ruler

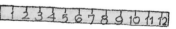

Here is what you do:

1. Cut the two longest fingers off the glove.

2. Cut a small slit about ½-inch (1¼-cm) from the tip of the shorter glove finger.

3. Slip the finger with the slit over the longer glove finger.

4. Break off the bowl ends of the two spoons. Leave a small handle tab on each one.

5. Cover the handle tabs with glue. Slip them into the slit on the top finger. Arrange them to look like two wings.

6. Glue on the wiggle eyes.

Put the puppet on your finger. Fly it around! Or try slipping it onto the handle of an electric toothbrush. Hear it buzz!

Fly-away Ladybug

Ladybugs' wing covers are
red with black spots.
The wing covers protect
the wings, which
are very thin.

Here is what you need:

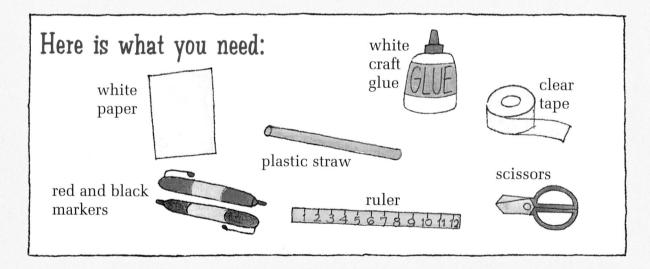

white
paper

white
craft
glue GLUE

clear
tape

plastic straw

red and black
markers

ruler
1 2 3 4 5 6 7 8 9 10 11 12

scissors

Here is what you do:

1. Cut a 2-inch (5-cm) circle from the paper.
You may need to trace around the bottom of a
cup first to get a good circle shape.

1 2 3 4 5 6 7 8 9 10 11 12

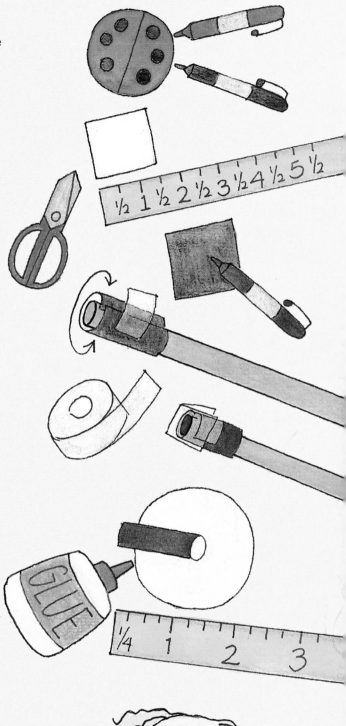

2. Use the markers to color the circle red with black dots.

3. Cut a 1½-inch (3¾-cm) square of paper.

4. Use the black marker to color one side of the paper.

5. Roll the paper around the end of the straw with the black side on the outside.

6. Secure the roll with tape. Make sure the paper roll slides on and off the straw easily.

7. Pinch the end of the roll. Tape it shut so no air can pass through. Use only a little tape.

8. Glue the red circle to the roll end so that ¼ inch (½ cm) of the black head sticks out beyond the ladybug's red body.

To "fly" the ladybug, blow on the open end of the straw. "Ladybug, ladybug, fly away home . . ."

17

Cluster of Moths Hairclip

Moths rest with their
wings spread out on
each side of their body.

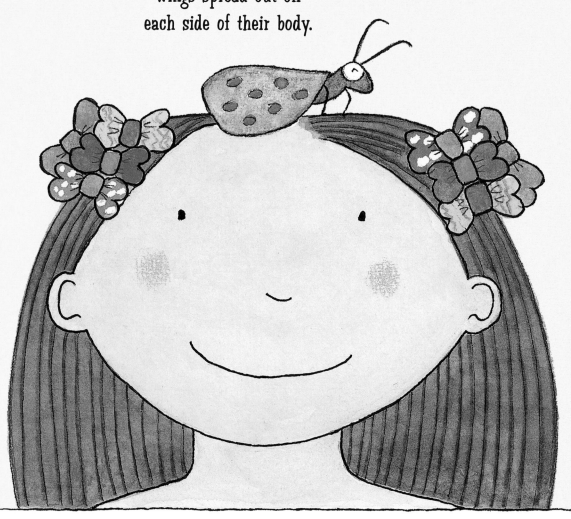

Here is what you need:

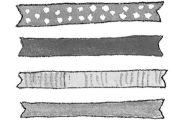

1- to 2-inch
(2½- to 5-cm) wide
printed and plain ribbons

hairclip

white
craft
glue

scissors

four or more
pony beads

ruler

Here is what you do:

1. Fold the ribbons in half lengthwise. Cut a rounded *M* shape out of the ribbon. Cut four or more shapes of different sizes. These will be the moth wings.

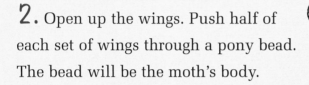

2. Open up the wings. Push half of each set of wings through a pony bead. The bead will be the moth's body.

3. Glue the moths together in a cluster.

4. Open the hairclip. Glue the cluster of moths on the front of the hairclip.

You can make this project into a pin by gluing the moths onto a pin back.

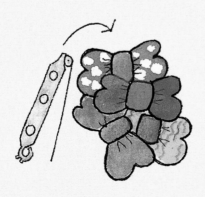

Hatching Caterpillar

Caterpillars hatch from eggs. Pop your very own caterpillar out of its egg with this project.

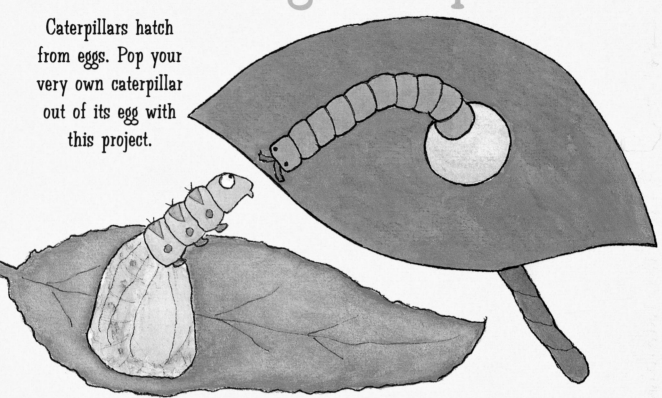

Here is what you need:

green felt

¾-inch (2-cm) wooden macramé bead with wide hole

scissors

black permanent marker

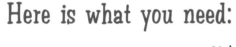

12-inch (30½-cm) green pipe cleaner

 ten green pony beads

ruler

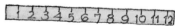

Here is what you do:

1. Cut a 6-inch (15-cm) leaf from the green felt.

2. Fold it in half. Cut a ¼-inch (½-cm) slit in the center. Fold it in half in the opposite direction. Cut a ¼-inch (½-cm) slit across the first cut.

3. Glue the bead to the leaf so the hole is over the cut.

4. Fold the green pipe cleaner in half. Thread the ten green pony beads over the pipe cleaner ends. Make sure the pony beads don't slide off the other end.

5. Bend the two ends over the last bead to keep it from sliding off. This bead will be the head.

6. Twist the remaining folded pipe cleaner to create a sturdy handle.

7. Use the black marker to draw eyes.

To hatch the caterpillar, hold the leaf and push the head up through the hole in the bead to look like it is coming out of an egg.

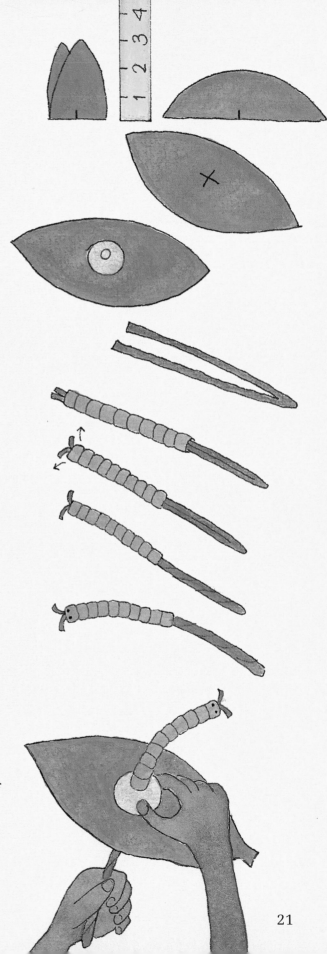

21

Caterpillar Pin

Moths, like butterflies, start out as caterpillars.
Create your own colorful caterpillar!

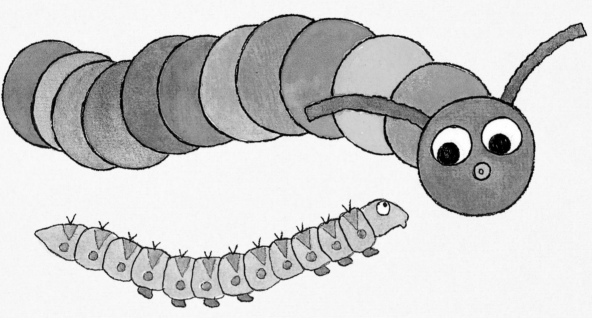

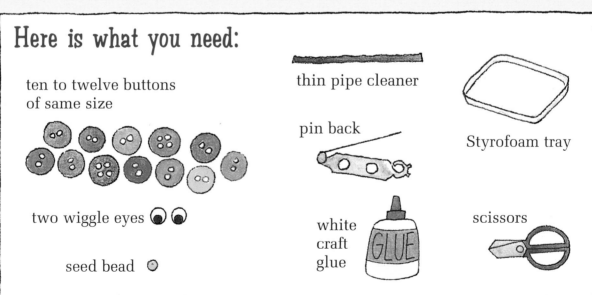

Here is what you need:

ten to twelve buttons
of same size

thin pipe cleaner

Styrofoam tray

pin back

two wiggle eyes

white
craft
glue

GLUE

scissors

seed bead

Here is what you do:

1. Working on the Styrofoam tray, glue the buttons together by overlapping them to form a long row of buttons.

2. Glue the two wiggle eyes to the front button.

3. Glue on the seed bead for a mouth.

4. Fold a piece of pipe cleaner in half to make the tentacles.

5. Glue the fold behind the button head.

6. Glue a pin back to the back of the caterpillar.

This pin would look great on your backpack or the collar of your jacket.

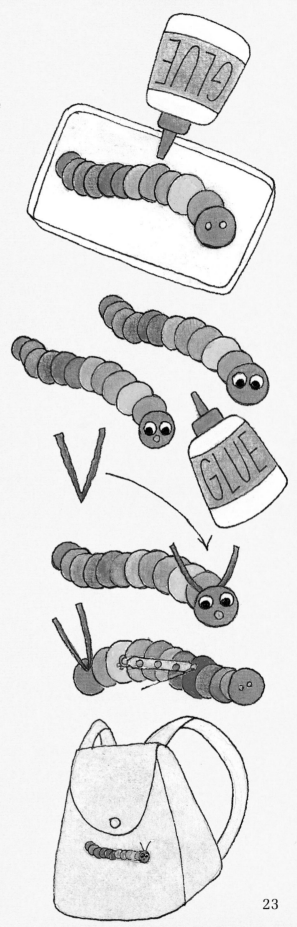

Emerging Butterfly

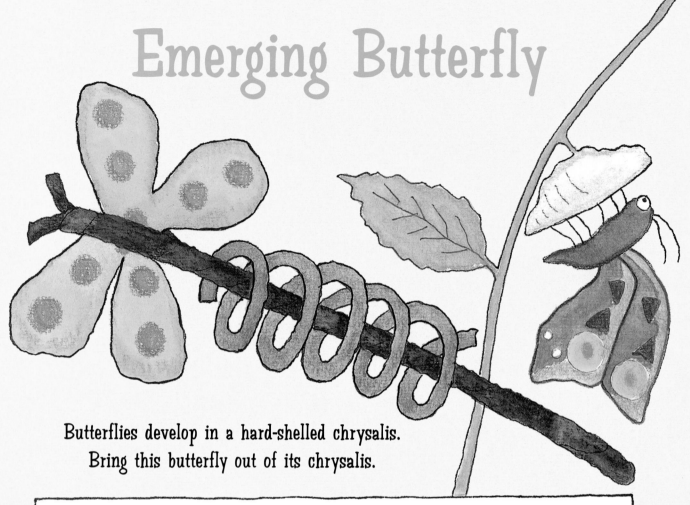

Butterflies develop in a hard-shelled chrysalis.
Bring this butterfly out of its chrysalis.

Here is what you need:

12-inch (30½-cm)
brown pipe cleaner

12-inch (30½-cm)
black pipe cleaner

fabric scrap

scissors

ruler

Here is what you do:

1. Fold the fabric scrap in half. Cut 2-inch
(5-cm) wide wings for the butterfly. Open
the folded fabric.

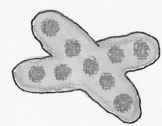

2. Fold the black pipe cleaner in half. Twist the two ends together with the tips bent out to form antennas.

3. Slip the center of the fabric wings between the pipe cleaners below the antennas. Twist the remainder of the pipe cleaner below the wings to secure the wings and create a tree branch.

4. Wrap the brown pipe cleaner loosely around your finger to create a chrysalis.

5. Slip the butterfly inside the chrysalis.

To use the puppet, push on the branch to make the butterfly emerge from the chrysalis. You might need to press down the ends of the pipe cleaner antennas to keep them from getting caught.

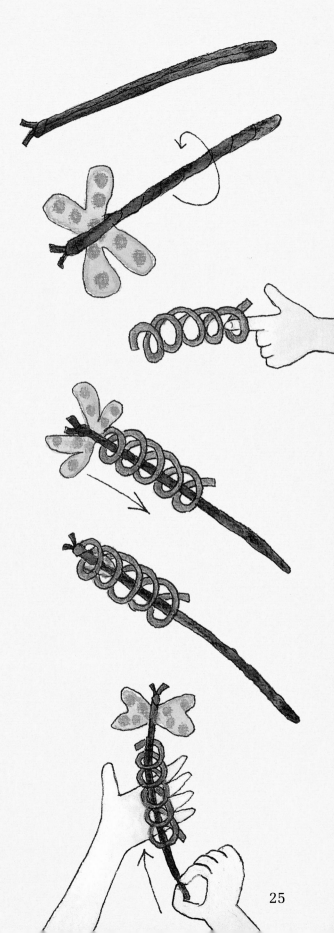

Fluttery Butterfly

Unlike their moth relatives, butterflies rest with their wings together over their back.

Here is what you need:

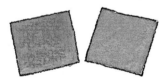

red (or another color) and green craft foam

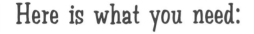

scissors

binder clip

6-inch (15-cm) black pipe cleaner

black permanent marker

white craft glue

Here is what you do:

1. Fold the pipe cleaner in half for the body.

2. Pinch the binder clip open. Glue the body inside.

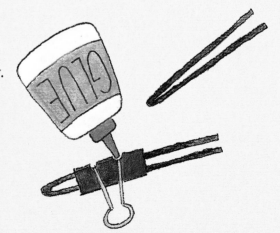

3. Spread the pipe cleaner ends to make the antennas. Trim off the extra.

4. Cut two wings from the craft foam.

5. Use the permanent marker to add details to the wings.

6. Glue a wing on each side of the clip.

7. Cut a leaf shape from the green craft foam, twice as long as the butterfly.

8. Cut a small slit in the center of the leaf.

9. Slip the ends of the clip down through the cut in the leaf.

Hold the project by the binder clip handles under the leaf. Pinch the handles to make the butterfly wings move.

Butterfly Wings Design

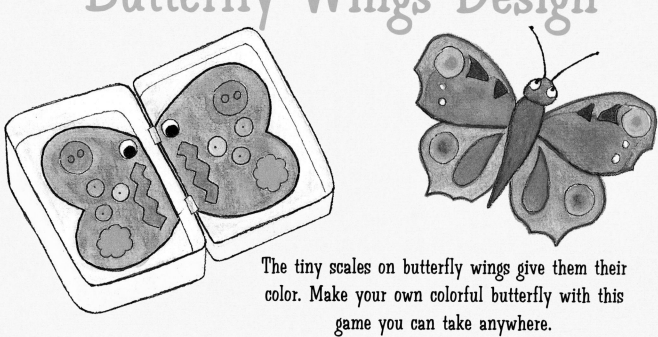

The tiny scales on butterfly wings give them their color. Make your own colorful butterfly with this game you can take anywhere.

Here is what you need:

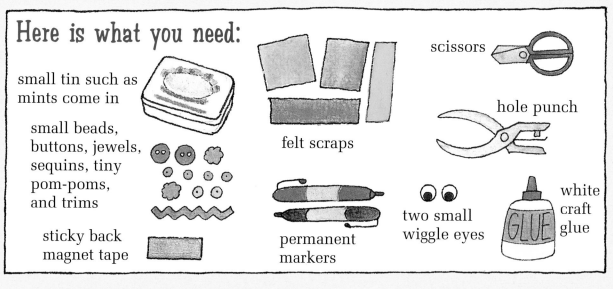

small tin such as mints come in

small beads, buttons, jewels, sequins, tiny pom-poms, and trims

sticky back magnet tape

felt scraps

permanent markers

two small wiggle eyes

scissors

hole punch

white craft glue

Here is what you do:

1. Open the tin box. Use the markers to draw a butterfly wings inside the lid and the base of the box.

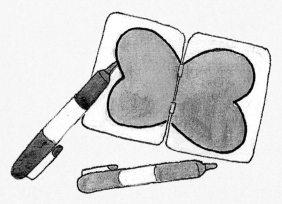

2. Punch several holes in the magnet.

3. Peel the paper off each magnet dot. Stick them to beads, sequins, buttons, craft jewels, tiny pom-poms, or pieces of trim. Make sets so you can make the wings match.

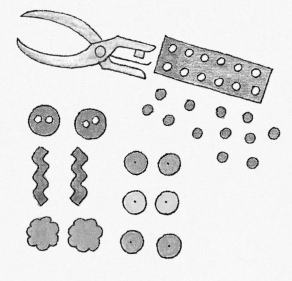

4. Punch two more holes. Stick them to the back of the wiggle eyes. Place the eyes to the top of the butterfly.

5. Cut a piece of felt to cover the lid. Glue the felt on the lid.

6. Cut a design or picture from the colorful felt scraps to glue on the lid.

Arrange the different pieces on each side of the butterfly to decorate the wings. You can add more pieces and trims to your butterfly game over time.

29

Butterfly Message Center

Butterflies carry pollen from one flower to another, but this butterfly delivers messages!

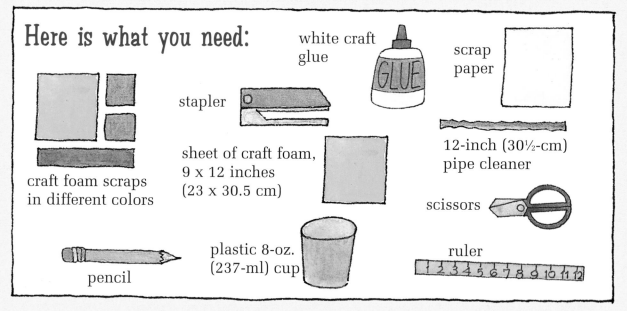

Here is what you need:

craft foam scraps in different colors

white craft glue

scrap paper

stapler

sheet of craft foam, 9 x 12 inches (23 x 30.5 cm)

12-inch (30½-cm) pipe cleaner

scissors

pencil

plastic 8-oz. (237-ml) cup

ruler

Here is what you do:

1. Fold the sheet of craft foam in half. Cut half a butterfly on the fold. Open the butterfly.

2. Cut upside down V shapes in the centers of the wing sections.

3. Fold the pipe cleaner in half. Slide it over the center of the butterfly wings.

4. Twist the two ends together to secure the pipe cleaner around the butterfly.

5. Spread out the two ends to form the antennas.

6. Decorate the wings of the butterfly by gluing on craft foam shapes.

7. Staple the butterfly to the side of the cup. Make sure the bottom of the wings does not hang below the bottom of the cup.

8. Cut 3-inch (8-cm) squares of scrap paper. Store them in the cup with a pencil.

Phone messages can be tucked into the Vs on the butterfly wings.

Ground Beetle Magnet

Ground beetles like to hide in moist places during the day. But this beetle would be happy to crawl up your fridge anytime.

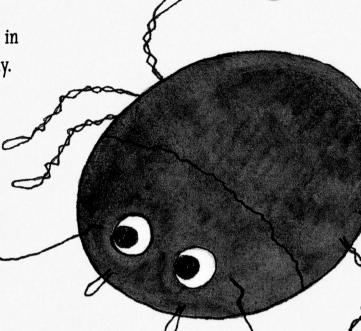

Here is what you need:

Styrofoam craft egg

two wiggle eyes

round craft magnet

9 thin black wire hairpins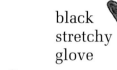

white craft glue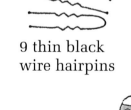

black stretchy glove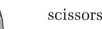

scissors

Here is what you do:

1. Ask a grownup to cut the Styrofoam craft egg in half lengthwise for you.

2. Cut the two longest fingers from the glove.

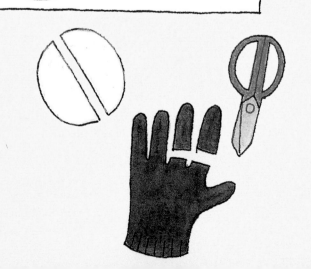

3. Pull one over each end of one of the egg halves. Overlap them to cover the egg. Secure with glue. This will be the beetle's body.

4. Pinch the hairpin together. Twist it to make a leg. Make six more.

5. Stick three legs into each side of the beetle.

6. Cut a hairpin in half at the fold. Stick one piece on each side of the head for the antennas.

7. Glue the wiggle eyes to the front of the beetle.

8. Pinch two more hairpins together. Twist them to make the pinchers. Push a pincher deep into each side of the head, below the eyes.

9. Glue the round magnet to the bottom of the beetle.

Post important messages or thank-you notes on the fridge!

Hi Mom! Thanks for the great lunch.

Flashing Firefly

Fireflies light up summer nights. You can flash this firefly any time you want!

Here is what you need:

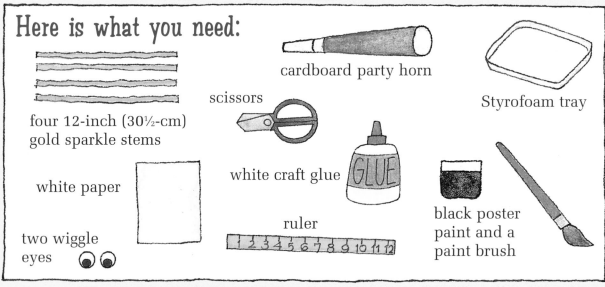

four 12-inch (30½-cm) gold sparkle stems

white paper

two wiggle eyes

scissors

white craft glue

ruler

cardboard party horn

Styrofoam tray

black poster paint and a paint brush

Here is what you do:

1. Working on the Styrofoam tray, paint the outside of the party horn. Paint about 2 inches (5 cm) up inside the horn. Let dry. This will be the firefly's body.

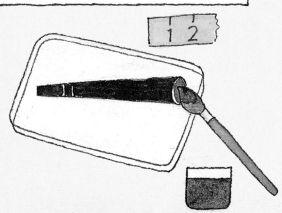

2. Glue the wiggle eyes to the horn's blower end.

3. Cut four wings from the paper. Glue two wings on each side of the back of the firefly.

4. Cut a small hole out of the bottom of the firefly about 3 inches (8 cm) from the open end.

5. Hold the four sparkle stems together. Fold them in half. Twist the fold together to form a handle.

6. Slide the folded end into the back of the firefly. Slide it through the cut opening. Bend it down slightly.

7. Spread the ends of the stems out slightly to resemble the firefly's rays of light.

To make the firefly puppet "flash," hold the body firmly with one hand. Push and pull the handle of the sparkle stems to move them in and out of the firefly.

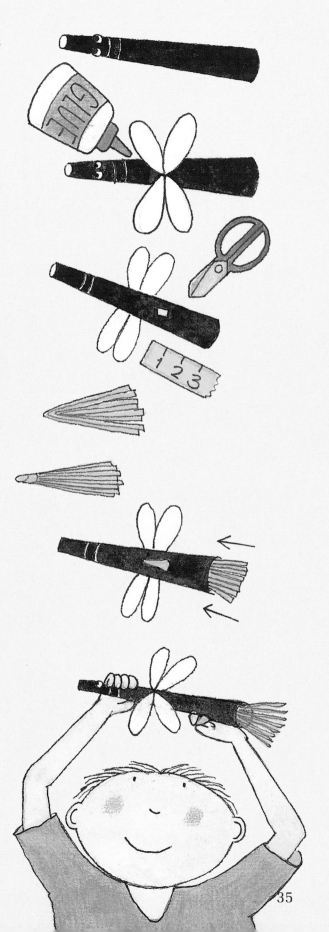

35

Ant Shaker

Even though it's hard to hear real ants, this ant can make noise in time to your favorite songs!

Here is what you need:

three tuna fish or pet food type cans, empty and clean

several buttons

scissors

two large wiggle eyes

four 12-inch (30½-cm) black pipe cleaners

black sock, adult-size

white craft glue

GLUE

ruler

1 2 3 4 5 6 7 8 9 10 11 12

Here is what you do:

1. Drop a few buttons in each of the three cans.

2. Slide the cans into the sock as far as they will go, end to end.

3. Wrap two 12-inch (30½-cm) pipe cleaners between the first and second cans. Bend the ends out on the bottom. Shape them into legs.

4. Wrap one 12-inch (30½-cm) pipe cleaner between the second and third cans. Bend the ends out on the bottom. Shape the last set of legs.

5. Close the end of the sock using a piece of pipe cleaner. Trim off the excess.

6. Cut a 6-inch (15-cm) piece of pipe cleaner.

7. Thread one end of the pipe cleaner through the sock at the top of the head to make the antennas.

8. Glue on the wiggle eyes.

"The ants go marching one by one . . ." Sing and shake!

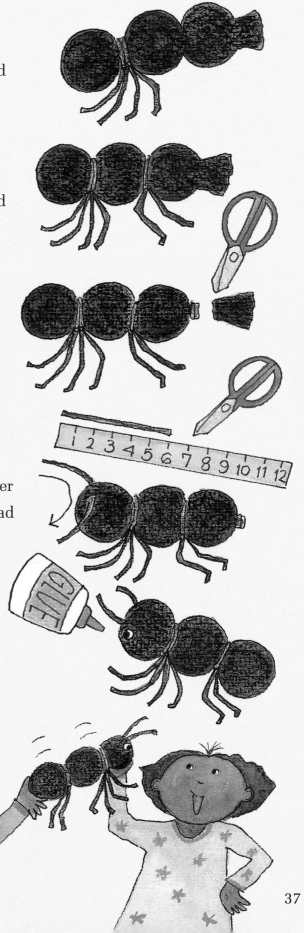

37

Cockroach Container

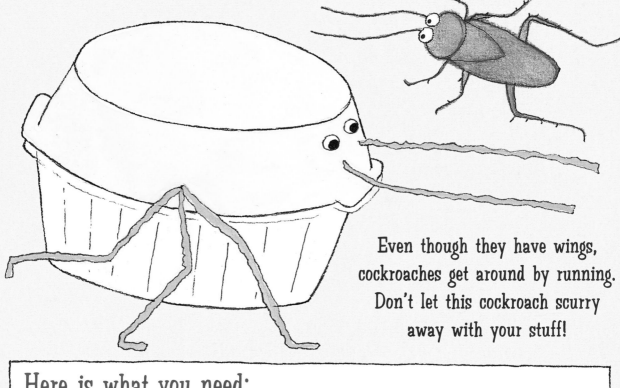

Even though they have wings, cockroaches get around by running. Don't let this cockroach scurry away with your stuff!

Here is what you need:

fast food baked potato container

two small wiggle eyes

white craft glue

four 12-inch (30½-cm) black pipe cleaners

Here is what you do:

1. Turn the container over so the foam bottom becomes the top.

2. Cut three pipe cleaners in half for the legs.

3. Poke the ends of three pipe cleaner halves through the top of each side of the container.

4. Fold over the ends inside the container.

5. Bend the centers of the pipe cleaners to form knees. Bend the ends out for the feet.

6. Glue the wiggle eyes to the front.

7. Thread the last pipe cleaner into the container, below the eyes. This pipe cleaner makes the antennas.

You can paint your cockroach container black or brown just like a real cockroach. Take the top off it, and stash stuff inside. Handy little fellow!

Dragonfly Bike Bopper

Real dragonflies can fly up to 35 miles (56 km) per hour. How fast will your dragonfly go riding on your handle bars?

Here is what you need:

two 12-inch (30½-cm) silver sparkle stems

green plastic straw

two wiggle eyes

white craft glue

scissors

two 12-inch (30½-cm) blue sparkle stems

two 12-inch (30½-cm) green sparkle stems

ruler

Here is what you do:

1. Twist one blue and one green sparkle stem together.

2. Fold the two ends of a silver sparkle stem into the center. Wrap to secure. This will be the wings. Make a second set of wings.

3. Fold the green and blue twisted sparkle stems in half. Place the center of the silver wings between the fold.

4. Twist the green and blue stems together on each side of the wings to form the body.

5. Trim the end of the body to 5 inches (13 cm) long.

6. Glue on the wiggle eyes.

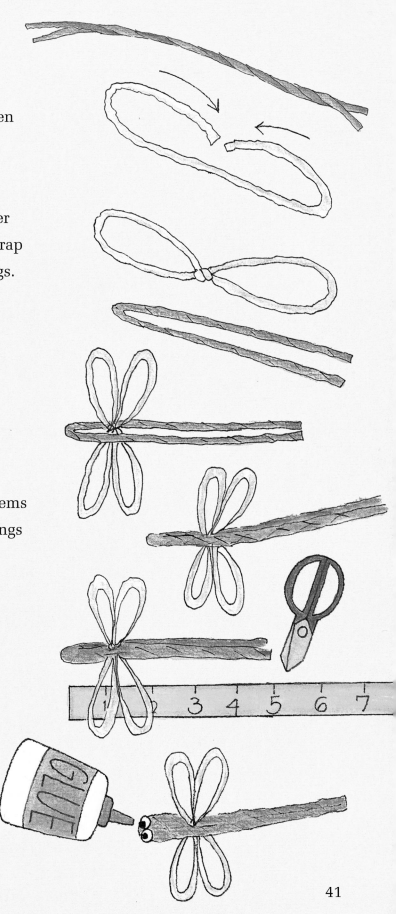

7. Twist the second blue and green sparkle stems together.

8. Attach one end of the twisted stems to the body, behind the wings.

9. Cut a 4-inch (10-cm) piece of straw.

10. Slip the piece over the twisted stems. Push it up to the dragonfly to stiffen the bobbing stem.

Attach the dragonfly to your bike by wrapping the end of the twisted stems around the handle bars. The dragonfly will bob and dart around when you take it for a ride.

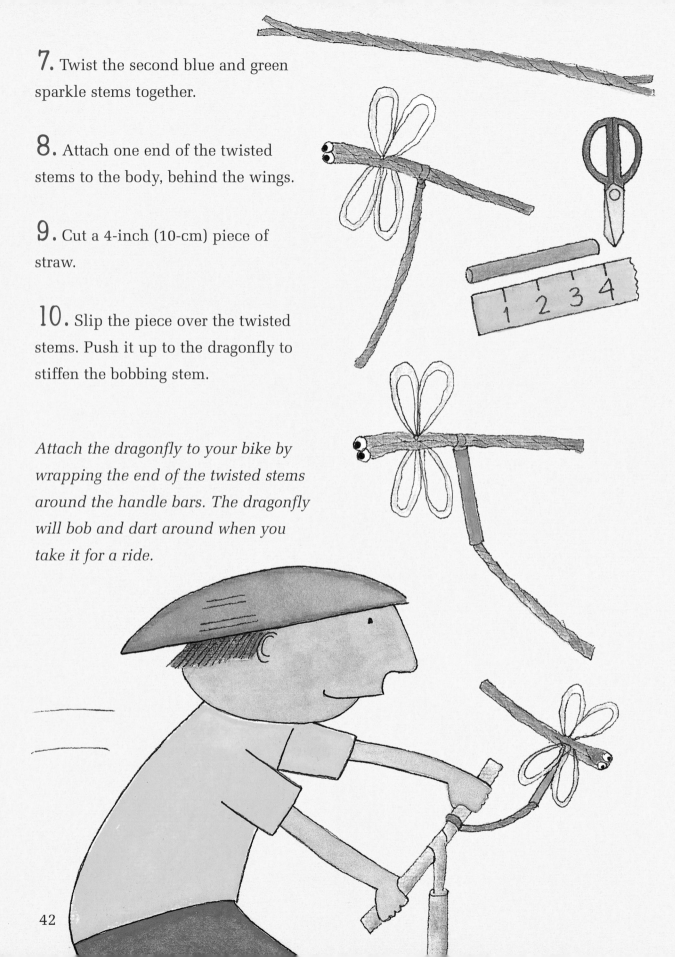

Quick Walking Stick

Walking Sticks are hard to spot because they blend into the twigs and sticks around them.

Here is what you need:

pencil

three twist ties

brown poster paint and a paintbrush

Styrofoam tray

two tiny wiggle eyes

Here is what you do:

1. Wrap the twist ties around the pencil to form legs.

2. Arrange the legs to make the walking stick stand.

3. Working on the Styrofoam tray, paint the walking stick brown. Let dry. If you plan to use the pencil for writing or erasing, do not paint the point or the eraser.

4. Glue on the wiggle eyes.

Walking Sticks move slowly to help them hide. Don't let your pencil walk away!

Hide the Bug Game

Some insects such as Katydids can be hard to see because they look like the plants near them.

Here is what you need:

two identical artificial leaves

green pony bead

white craft glue

two brown seed beads

stiff string or thin wire

two 12-inch (30½-cm) green pipe cleaners

ruler

scissors

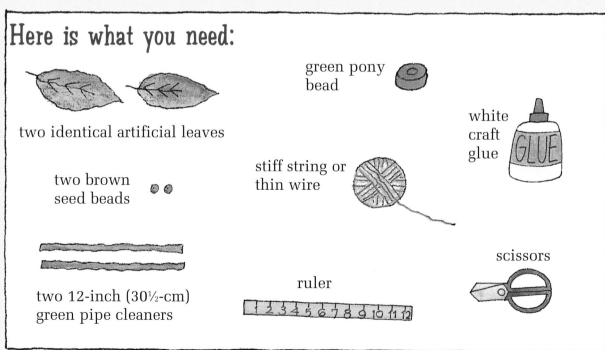

Here is what you do:

1. Cut three 6-inch (15-cm) pieces of the green pipe cleaner.

2. Fold each piece in half. Fold each end out to the side, down, and out again to shape legs.

3. Glue the backs of the two leaves together with the fold of the legs between them. Glue the pony bead to the stem end of the leaves.

4. Fold a 2-inch (5-cm) piece of stiff string or wire in half. Cover the fold with glue. Slip it between the two leaves.

5. Glue two seed beads to the head for eyes.

You and your friends can take turns hiding this insect and your homemade Walking Sticks outside for the others to search for.

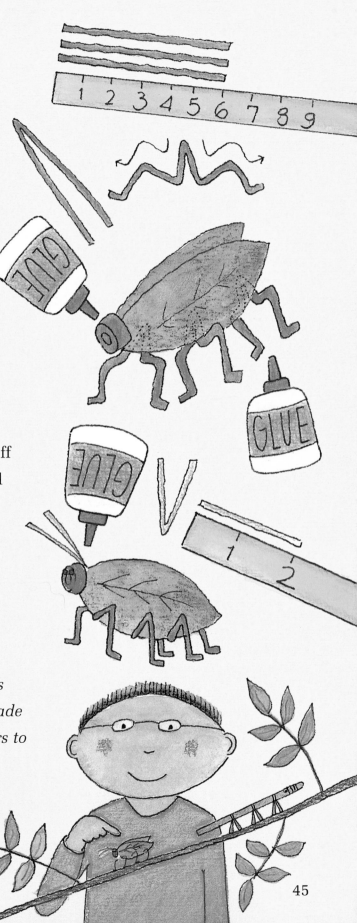

45

The Termite Game

Because termites like to eat wood,
they can damage homes.

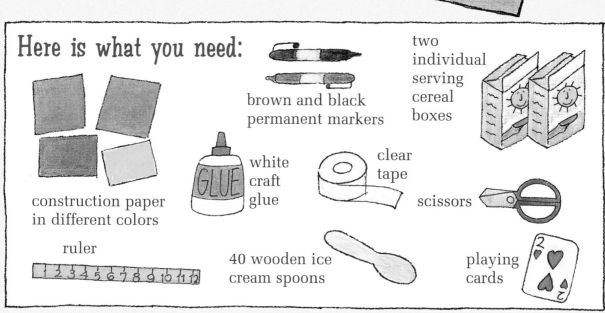

Here is what you need:

brown and black
permanent markers

two
individual
serving
cereal
boxes

construction paper
in different colors

white
craft
glue

clear
tape

scissors

ruler

1 2 3 4 5 6 7 8 9 10 11 12

40 wooden ice
cream spoons

playing
cards

Here is what you do:

1. Use the markers to add details to the wooden
spoons to make each one look like a termite.

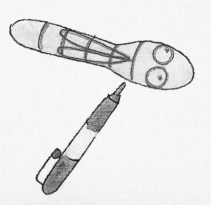

2. Open one flap from each cereal box. Then cut off enough of the flap to leave a ⅛-inch (¼-cm) slit.

3. Close the flaps. Tape them, leaving a narrow slot large enough for one termite spoon to slip through.

4. Wrap the sides of the box with construction paper. Secure with the tape.

5. Cut windows, a door, and a triangle roof for each box from the construction paper. Glue the pieces in place.

6. Use the markers to add window panes and a door knob.

How to play the game:

Play the game with a friend. Each person will need a house with 20 termite spoons inside. Take the 2s, 3s, and 4s from the deck of cards plus one 6 card. Mix them up. Place them in a pile in the center. Take turns drawing a card. The number on the card is the number of times you get to shake the house to try to get a termite out. If you shake the house more times than the card allows, you must put all your termites back in your house. The first person to get out all the termites is the winner.

When you have termites in the house, you want to get rid of them fast!

About the Author and Artist

Thirty years as a teacher and director of nursery school programs have given Kathy Ross extensive experience in guiding young children through crafts projects. Among the more than forty craft books she has written are **Crafts For All Seasons**, **More of the Best Holiday Crafts Ever**, **The Storytime Craft Book**, and the **All New Holiday Crafts for Kids** series. You can find out more about Kathy's books by visiting her at www.Kathyross.com

Jan Barger, originally from Little Rock, Arkansas, now lives in Plumpton, East Sussex, England, with her husband and their cocker spaniel, Tosca. She has written and illustrated a number of children's books and is known for her gentle humor and warm, friendly characters. She also designs greeting cards, sings with the Brighton Festival Chorus, and plays piccolo with the Sinfonia of Arun.

Together, Kathy and Jan have written and illustrated the **Learning is Fun** series.